Slow Wind

poems by

Joshua Hamilton

Finishing Line Press
Georgetown, Kentucky

Slow Wind

Copyright © 2016 by Joshua Hamilton
ISBN 978-1-944251-89-5 First Edition
All rights reserved under International and Pan-American Copyright Conventions. No part of this book may be reproduced in any manner whatsoever without written permission from the publisher, except in the case of brief quotations embodied in critical articles and reviews.

ACKNOWLEDGMENTS

I am deeply grateful to my wife, Leticia Bajuyo, whose optimism and inexhaustible energy always motivate me when I feel depleted and defeated. She has helped me invaluably in the development of my creative eye and my aesthetic philosophy, and our conversations together have helped me mature as a thinker and as a human. I owe a great debt to Melissa Dinverno for pushing me to think deeper about poetic and aesthetic questions, and for guiding me through the exhaustive process of revision. My daughter, Aida Beth, has shown me what it means to perceive the world through the senses again, reminding me of the magical dimensions inherent to every day life. My family has been a bulwark of encouragement and strength through everything I have endeavored, and I owe them—my parents Elizabeth and James Hamilton, my siblings Ellen Campbell, Elizabeth Meshkoff, and Mark Hamilton—a great debt of gratitude. I also have to thank my home of five years, Madison, IN, for reminding me what it means to take a long walk through an old town and look at my world carefully and slowly. And I sincerely appreciate Kay Stokes, for being a reader for me and giving me much needed mentorship, and Leah Maines, Christen Kincaid, and Finishing Line Press for bringing these poems into their fold.

Editor: Christen Kincaid

Cover Art: Joshua Bridgwater Hamilton

Author Photo: Leticia Bajuyo

Cover Design: Elizabeth Maines

Printed in the USA on acid-free paper.
Order online: www.finishinglinepress.com
          also available on amazon.com

                Author inquiries and mail orders:
                      Finishing Line Press
                        P. O. Box 1626
                  Georgetown, Kentucky 40324
                            U. S. A.

Table of Contents

1. Sound of wind and leaves 1
2. Twenty-first century perspective 2
3. A fedora with feather 3
4. A mess of starlings at twilight 4
5. Before morning 5
6. The giveaway sweepstakes 6
7. A few put faith in me 7
8, A spittle of road 8
9. I had forgotten how many phases 9
10. First thought after dream 10
11. Warm winter morning 11
12. I stare at my teeth in the mirror 12
13. Material 13
14. I confuse Drosophilidae 14
15. Slow wind at my back 15
16. Departures, arrivals 16
17. Awake in the middle of night 17
18. Harsh icy morning 19
19. Several months ago 20
20. A dog smacks the glass 21
21. Afternoon nap 22
22. On this relentless journey 23
23. The flickering oil of memory 24
24. Overeating, lassitude, distraction 25
25. Against dark windows 26
26. Wait until 27
27. Road north 28
28. To reinterpret the same leaves 29

For Letty and Aida Beth

1.

Sound of wind and leaves
tumbles through the rafters
Sunday morning—
an old warmth and simplicity
scratching against this anxious shell
of cramped minutes, toddler perils, and late work:
a memory of a squat cottage
on the outskirts—
smoky curl and brown-green carpet
of leaves and grass,
the streaked white-blue
of cloud and sky
on the cusp between autumn and winter
that frames the scarred door—
a door in my mind opened obsessively
in adolescence
but abandoned twenty years later.
I find this cottage again, as in a dream,
and cross the yard, but the dwelling remains
out of reach as I walk and walk
towards it.

2.

Twenty-first century perspective:
cloud settings to pierce landscapes
and bring out highlights—
silver linings
in a fog of allergens
while we plant new gardens
with chemical blooms and sunflower screens.
I want to be like photos,
their proof sheet
spilling out from mouse clics
like water from a stabbed water balloon—
each brief image samples
or suggests a photo's potential:
an object committed to being object,
that bares its surface
to the tattoo parlor of human
inscription and history—
torn paper against the palm,
inked comments and names
smeared across the back.

3.

A fedora with feather
used in a thousand dream-winning,
tilted-brim gestures
by a 1960s man, a 19
50s 40s 30s man
when the bash of the crown
the smooth grain of the felt
and the grosgrain band
introduced the wearer.
Up for auction,
I bid on the lesson learned—
frugality captured in the sweatband,
the beat-up and busted crown,
stains on the ribbon
and mothbites in the worn felt;
I bid on the artful,
the artefault,
and win, and bid,
and win,
until I have to build a walk-in closet
to store all these lessons of frugality.

4.

A mess of starlings at twilight
chatters up the bony canopy,
up limbs still poised from the autumn
strip-tease.
Electric lights and computer signals
crimp my thoughts,
unsettled—
flitting from branch
                to
                      branch—
a constant physics whipped up
by hard-drive hums, password queries,
and lost searches—the forgotten fields
of a user left prodding
and poking into thin air—
the key just hidden by visual illusion...
                a glimmer
                      that catches
my tiny, obsidian eye:
beyond these sparkling vistas—
a raucous
storm of starlings
beats wind into the trees
shaking the perimeter into sudden clouds,
lifting, exploding
across the morning.

5.

Before morning
broken frames
and torn portraits clatter in the attic.
Loose joints and crude stairs,
steeply ascending space without balustrade,
tremble with the pressure
of a forgotten flood, a desert ocean
pummeling dreamed memories
and blasting the rot, stink,
bacterial implosion of moldering ancient
structure
that smothers faces and past lives
whose vague traces struggle
to imprint in the dust.
The sun rises, then, with a blank smile,
toasts the world beneath
without a lick of irony.

6.

The giveaway sweepstakes: allure
of an object, consumable,
that draws me in—to enter
I reproduce the company info
on my Facebook page,
my Twitter feed,
I become
their commercial.
Driving along the state road today,
I saw a squirrel
disappear under the car
without even a thump;
no sign of it in the rear views,
as if it were swept up,
absorbed by the complex
machinery of the vehicle.

7.

A few put faith in me—
a gut expectation
grounded in diurnal optimism.
I take it from them,
more dehydrated than I know,
even delirious,
and deliriously give a little—
token strawberries,
slippery bites
I didn't plan on eating.
In the end, though,
comes the orange and brown autumn
to distract me:

when I wander off,
no one comes looking.

8.

A spittle of road
augured into a block of night
by headlights
and wound with constant echoes
of death—it cupped
my car with fickle,
ancient attentions:
fate distracted by the deer about to lunge
the passing car in the oncoming lane
or the fog-enshrouded curve.

9.

I had forgotten how many phases the night has
until my daughter reminded me:
one for the dimming, after the rattle
of silverware settles in the drying rack;
one for the stories, as the pages shuffle
and the voices drone;
one for the adults
in the later yellow lamp glow,
as they wonder at the hollow that quickly dwindles
in the pit of night;
and one for after all
when even lost dreams have gotten tired
and laid their delirium down.

10.

First thought after dream:
"rain."
Soft curling breath next to me:
seedpod
with lungs and limbs
sprouted warm in the hollow of sleep,
a quiet lightning in body and brain
that skitters during day hours
over linoleum, carpet, and dirt,
and prods infinite connections
that only seem veiled to me,
but to her, manifest the only
legible writing in the world.

11.

Warm winter morning
brings misty weather
to smear the town streets
and the valleys gray.
The river noodles southwest—
news reports
barges colliding near New Orleans.
I dip my finger in the current
and feel the oil slickening
a thousand miles downstream.
The deep carve of water
bears its geo-giant blade
down on the river bottom
in cosmically slow motion
as the stink of river mud
and rotten leaves
rises up through the haze
of a warm winter morning.

12.

I stare at my teeth in the mirror—
the blades of the carnivore's mouth:
yellowed from age, tobacco, coffee;
worn down from grinding and eating—
in the molar depressions, dark
mineral deposits accrete:
tablets, tombstones, ivory parapets
on which the organic history of one mouth
has been engraved in defense, erasure,
and consumption of death.

13.

Material
disintegrates slowly:
mortar, brick, plywood, sheetrock,
pressed metal and plastics,
paper and cloth:
colors fade from the surface of books, walls and tables—
no time or wherewithal
to counter the decay of property
and autobiography:
I've been too busy rereading
the same moldering paragraph
these past 10 years,
and I cannot close the book,
though it has cost me everything.

14.

I confuse Drosophilidae
with Tephritidae—
one lingers around rotten fruit,
the other feasts on unripe fruit.
A fistula forms between the two facts—
parallel faulty information
balanced in a working relationship.

15.

Slow wind at my back;
the serious rooster and crow
scrabble at their shadows,
but dawn shrouded and blinded me
before I myself could crow or peck.
She's quiet, forbearing:
anger and pleasure equal in the patient
cascading procession
of opaque curtains.
My exaggerated resolutions
furl away a lifetime
of listless effort;
yet here dawn comes again—
blinds and nudges,
slow wind at my back.

16.

Departures, arrivals
accumulate like a collection
of ribbons—little strips
torn from memory,
wrinkle-smoothed and tattered
at both ends:
wake up, percolate,
knot a tie and drive a while...
then nothing.
A collapsed thread
between here and there.
Classes taught, baths given,
bottles opened—
under the influence
of a suspended perception
I collect scraps
wishing for chapters:
matinal fog blurs
the scattered businesses along the street,
small gaps on Main,
then farmhouses,
carpets of corn
and soybean—a dimmed
landscape
blotted out by the sharp detail
and proximity
of the car's cabin.

17.

Awake in the middle of night,
I listen to the central air
playing its blustery lullaby;
everyone quiet while my pen bleeds out—
its thorough black and blue
obliterate the blank calm
as I desperately staunch
a flood of gasping, sodden habits...
People do amazing and horrific things;
some do nothing;
others, their whole lives,
draw blueprints for clouds,
ransom their daily allotment
of credit
for the nervy tinctures of night.
I think about the vehicle
that dropped me off nowhere
in the middle of my life:
sleek, transparent, commercially
fluid—its narrative moves
through all landscapes,
unimpeded by geography
or physics.
On the pavement where it left me
a weak powdering of snow—
its fine dust reduces the vast
plain behind me
to blank parchment.
Before me, a broken-down joint
flush with hot orange light
leaky slats,

an empty bar and a full house
of keening, over-
whelming sound.
As I walk through the door,
I hand over my last
line of credit.

18.

Harsh icy morning
breaks across my brow,
turns the jelly of my eyes
to deep bruised blue.
Against this early shiver
I grab rope,
lean out to the horizon—
a cluttered convex
sucked up and spit out
by jagged rust, splintered wood,
a thousand shipwrecks
through which mine,
like an icebreaker
in the arctic,
labors,
yard
by shrieking
yard.

19.

Several months ago
I stopped cutting the dead
that sprout from my scalp.
Eventually, the corpse part of me
simply split ends, frizzed,
and curled into crazy
silhouettes.
The dead grow long now,
and fall in cascading waves—
the weight, the unruly
medieval locks
remind me that, sometimes,
we confuse trimming the dead
with staying alive.

20.

A dog smacks the glass
of a storm door
with his treble spatter;
the sky dumps on grassland
its heavy recycled load,
then lingers, irrigating sorrowfully
all weekend long.
The irritants and inundations
sweep me away—if I were stronger,
steadier,
then the hull of my life wouldn't breach,
like the cruise ships and oil rigs
listing at sea
their shipwrecks dredged up daily
in the news:
a dream variation
on sleeping sacs and log cabins
as the next thousand years
rustle in the tree limbs.

21.

Afternoon nap:
orange glow from curtains,
humming fan—additions
of sense inducement
I set up with the care
of a hypnotist
leading my daughter to sopor.
The spell too strong,
I lie down west side of the bed,
parallel to her
and drift—
neurotic layers crinkle away,
shed like wax paper
from a taffy,
or tissue paper from a gift—
the only possession in existence
is that packet of sleep
wedged between noon
and dinner.

22.

On this relentless journey
headlights open up
a short road before us—
not even moon or snowy countryside
lighten the dark strip where a sudden shimmer
warns of ice.
I drive and obsess:
daughter strapped behind me—
little egg in a 70
mile-an-hour crate;
the mother beside me—
fresh spat still crackling between.
Meanwhile, I tie my stomach into knots
around all that frightens me,
try not to swerve
over the ghost-black ice.

23.

The flickering oil of memory
floats a single flame in inky waters
spread from the dual current
of labor and leisure,
haunts the folded dawns
tucked within technological reveries—
a paradox of temperatures
within a frantic fever:
the blue calm gutters
imperceptibly
in the plastics and petrol of the past,
insistent, making misery
of the sizzling present.

24.

Overeating, lassitude, distraction—
slippage of family vacation:
the mind's eye knocked hard,
autofocus broken...
we take hurried images of life
and dump them in the blank
electronic nether
of the brain's infinite,
synaptic space.

25.

Against dark windows
on the bare-skinned hour
autumn falls.
Bedtime: the baby
skims surfaces, dipping
into the perverse ocean
of humanity—
her soft chest to the raw
flood of destiny
intoned with hurricane blasts
of sound, motion, image;
awareness finally dwindles
and quiet descends
to the tympanic vestibule
where the delicate timbre
of fear
registers.

26.

Wait until it
barely makes sense,
then act
as though you were made for it—
designer at the gates of dawn,
broker at a power lunch—
let no one know you lie,
especially yourself;
it takes courage to be a coward
and persistence to be weak.
Where the fierce and loyal
gather round the totem pole
before the sitcom season starts
you'll find the deepest current
of affinities—
the tribes with sunned arms
and scars dug in their skin;
time to infiltrate
and move through them.

27.

Road north—pine trees,
farm plots framed by hedge rows;
sun on the left
warms the uneven geometries
disturbed by the rhythm of wheel
against road.
Sheep form perfect clouds
in the expectant plots.
Clear away the trash,
leave the weeds, frame up
the sun-scorched abandonment:
parking lots and crops
unfold a peculiar lyric—old paint lines
cracked and bleeding green,
hard work from five decades ago
redistributed
in natural resource.
Meanwhile, flake-painted motorcycles
pass by, tiny earthquakes
from chromed gems—
garish as the original paint
on Greek statues.
Impeccable symmetries
and violent colors
have replaced the shrines
of antiquity: interrogated,
incinerated,
by a perpetual v-thumping.

28.

To reinterpret the same leaves that rustle by on the daily drive,
remember the common passages easily forgotten,
reflect both sharp and dull in the same glance;

To find new systems in the rote,
create new experience hiking the same path—
or simply walk attentively through the mind,

observing
and inverting
in the same stride.

Joshua Hamilton is a Louisville, KY native living in Madison, IN, with his family: artist Leticia Bajuyo, daughter Aida Beth Bajuyo-Hamilton, and two cats, Capitán and Walnut. He earned his Bachelor's in English and Humanities and his Master's in Spanish from the University of Louisville, and in 2013 he completed his doctorate in Spanish (with a minor in American Literature) with Indiana University.

www.ingramcontent.com/pod-product-compliance
Lightning Source LLC
Chambersburg PA
CBHW060225050426
42446CB00013B/3177